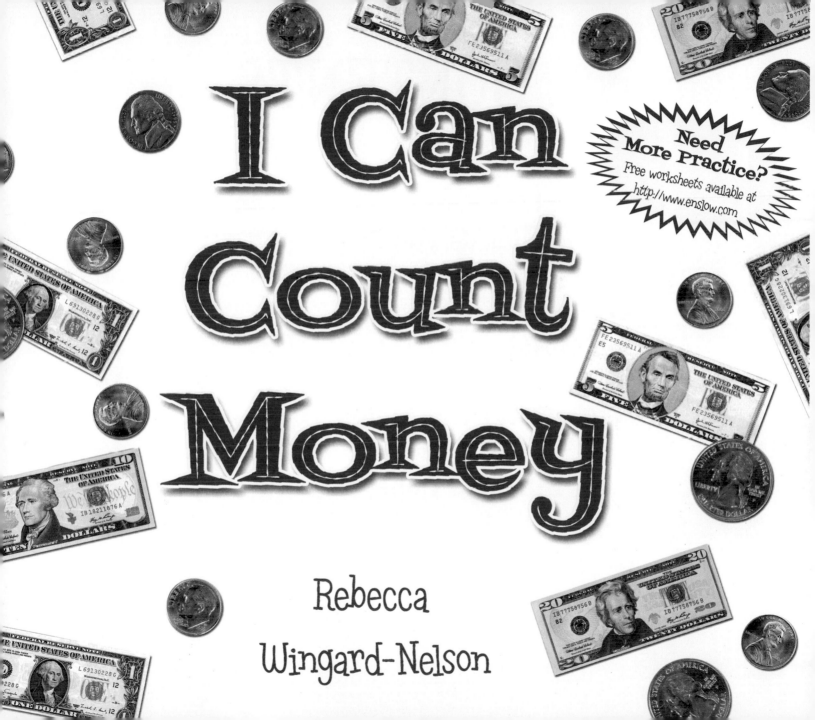

I Can Count Money

Rebecca

Wingard-Nelson

CONTENTS

Coins and Bills. 3

Counting Like Coins. 4

Counting Nickels and Pennies 6

Counting With Dimes 8

Counting With Quarters 10

Make an Amount 12

Least Number of Coins. 14

Counting Over One Dollar 16

Counting Bills 18

Bills and Coins Together 20

Let's Review. 22

Learn More

Books. 23

Web Sites 23

Index 24

Coins and Bills

penny
1¢

nickel
5¢

dime
10¢

quarter
25¢

one-dollar bill
$1

five-dollar bill
$5

ten-dollar bill
$10

twenty-dollar
bill
$20

Counting Like Coins

You can count to find the value of a group of coins.

One penny = 1¢
Count pennies by ones.

Ten pennies = 10¢

1¢   2¢   3¢   4¢   5¢

6¢   7¢   8¢   9¢   10¢

One nickel = 5¢
Count nickels by fives.

5¢   10¢   15¢   20¢   25¢

Five nickels = 25¢

One dime = 10¢
Count dimes by tens.

10¢   20¢   30¢   40¢   50¢

Five dimes = 50¢

One quarter = 25¢
Count quarters twenty-fives.

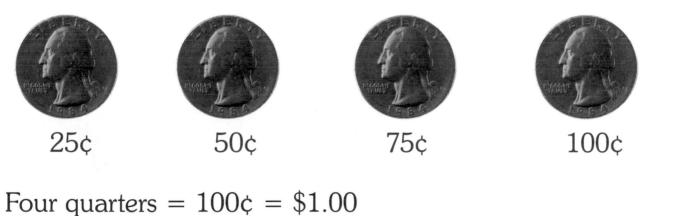

25¢   50¢   75¢   100¢

Four quarters = 100¢ = $1.00

Counting Nickels and Pennies

One way to count the value of different kinds of coins is to count the most valuable coins first. Count nickels before pennies.

Find the value of 1 nickel and 3 pennies.

Count the nickel first. 5¢

5¢

Now count one more for each penny.
5¢, 6¢, 7¢, 8¢

7¢

The value of the coins is 8¢.   6¢   8¢

Find the value of 3 nickels and 2 pennies.

Count by fives for the nickels.
5¢, 10¢, 15¢

5¢ 10¢

15¢

Now count one more
for each penny.
15¢, 16¢, 17¢

16¢

17¢

The value of the coins is 17¢.

Counting With Dimes

Find the value of 1 dime and 2 nickels.

Count the dime first. 10¢

10¢

Now count five more
for each nickel.
10¢, 15¢, 20¢

15¢

The value of the coins is 20¢.

20¢

Find the value of 2 dimes, 1 nickel, and 4 pennies.

You can count dimes first, then nickels, then pennies.

Count by 10s for the dimes.
10¢, 20¢

Then count five more for the nickel. 20¢, 25¢

Then count one more for each penny.
25¢, 26¢, 27¢, 28¢, 29¢

The value of the coins is 29¢.

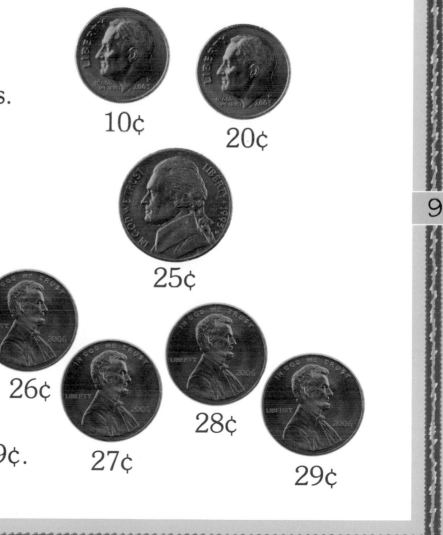

10¢

20¢

25¢

26¢

27¢

28¢

29¢

Counting With Quarters

Find the value of 1 quarter and 2 dimes.

You can count the quarter first. 25¢

25¢

Then count ten more
for each dime.
25¢, 35¢, 45¢

35¢

45¢

The value of the coins is 45¢.

Find the value of 2 quarters, 2 dimes, 2 nickels, and 1 penny.

You can count quarters first. Count by 25s. 25¢, 50¢

Count ten more for each dime. 50¢, 60¢, 70¢

Count five more for each nickel. 70¢, 75¢, 80¢

Count one more for the penny. 80¢, 81¢

The value of the coins is 81¢.

25¢

50¢

60¢

70¢

75¢

80¢

81¢

Make an Amount

You can use coins to make a given amount.

What coins can you use to make 76¢?

Three quarters make 75¢.

25¢

50¢

75¢

One penny more makes 76¢.

76¢

Three quarters and one penny make 76¢.

What other coins could you use to make 76¢?

Seven dimes make 70¢.

10¢   20¢   30¢

40¢   50¢   60¢   70¢

One nickel more makes 75¢.

One penny more makes 76¢.

75¢

76¢

Seven dimes, one nickel, and one penny make 76¢.

Least Number of Coins

To make an amount using the least number of coins, you can use the most valuable coins first.

Make 37¢ using the least number of coins possible.

Can you use any quarters?
One quarter is 25¢.
25¢ is less than 37¢.
Two quarters are 50¢.
50¢ is more than 37¢.
Use only one quarter.

Can you use any dimes?
You have 25¢ from the quarter.
One dime more makes 35¢.
35¢ is less than 37¢.
Another dime makes 45¢.
45¢ is more than 37¢.
Use only one dime.

25¢   50¢

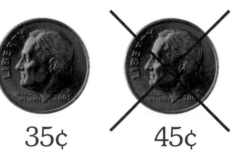

35¢   45¢

Can you use any nickels?
You have 35¢ from the
quarter and dime.
One nickel more makes 40¢.
40¢ is more than 37¢
Do not use any nickels.

40¢

Can you use any pennies?
You have 35¢ from the
quarter and dime.
One penny more makes 36¢.
36¢ is less than 37¢.
Another penny makes 37¢. Stop.
37¢ is the amount you want to make. Use two pennies.

36¢   37¢

The least number of coins to
make 37¢ is these four coins:
1 quarter, 1 dime, and 2 pennies.

25¢   35¢   36¢   37¢

Counting Over One Dollar

Money values can be written using a dollar sign and a decimal point.

dollar sign   decimal point

$1.37

1 dollar   37 cents

Numbers on the left side of the decimal point stand for dollars.

Numbers on the right side of the decimal point stand for cents.

When you say a money amount, say the dollars first. Say "and" at the decimal point. Then say the cents. $1.62 is read "one dollar and sixty-two cents."

Find the value of 5 quarters and 1 penny.

Let's count the values out loud.

25¢
Say "twenty-five cents."

50¢
Say "fifty cents."

75¢
Say "seventy-five cents."

100¢ = $1.00
Say "one dollar."

$1.25
Say "one dollar and twenty-five cents."

$1.26
Say "one dollar and twenty-six cents."

The value of the coins is $1.26.

Counting Bills

Count the value of bills the same way you count coins. You can count the most valuable bills first.

Find the value of the bills shown.

Count the twenty-dollar bills first. There is one. Count 20. The total value so far is $20.00.

Count the ten-dollar bills. There are three. Start with 20 from the twenty-dollar bill. Count ten more for each bill. Count 20, 30, 40, 50. The total value so far is $50.00.

Count the five-dollar bills.
There is one. Start with 50
for the bills already counted.
Count five more for each bill.
Count 50, 55.
The total value so far is $55.00.

Count the one-dollar bills.
There are four. Start with 55
for the bills already counted.
Count one more for each bill.
Count 55, 56, 57, 58, 59.

The total value of the bills is $59.00.

Bills and Coins Together

Chris has 1 ten-dollar bill, 2 one-dollar bills, 2 quarters, and 1 nickel in his pocket. How much money is in his pocket?

Bills and coins are sometimes counted together by counting the bills first, then the coins. The most valuable bill in Chris's pocket is the ten-dollar bill.

Count 10 for the ten-dollar bill.

10

There are two one-dollar bills.
Start with 10 from the ten-dollar bill.
Count one more for each bill.
Count 10, 11, 12.

11

There are no more bills.
The total value of the bills is $12.00.

12

Count the value of the coins.

Count 25¢ for each quarter.
There are two. Count 25¢, 50¢.

Count five more for the nickel.
Count 50¢, 55¢.

There are no more coins.
The total value of the coins is 55¢.

25¢   50¢

55¢

Write the value of the bills and coins together
using a dollar sign and a decimal point.
Write the dollars on the left side of the
decimal point, and the cents on the right.

$12.55

dollars   cents

$12.55 is read "twelve dollars and fifty-five cents."

Chris has $12.55 in his pocket.

LET'S REVIEW

The value of a set of coins can be found by counting.

Count the value of pennies by 1s.
1¢, 2¢, 3¢, 4¢, . . .

Count the value of nickels by 5s.
5¢, 10¢, 15¢, 20¢, . . .

Count the value of dimes by 10s.
10¢, 20¢, 30¢, 40¢, . . .

Count the value of quarters by 25s.
25¢, 50¢, 75¢, . . .

One way to find the value of a set of mixed coins is to count the coins with the greatest value first. Count quarters, then dimes, then nickels, then pennies.

To write dollars and cents together, use a dollar sign and a decimal point.

$12.55

dollars   cents

LEARN MORE

Books

Dalton, Julie. *Counting Money*. New York: Children's Press, 2006.

Kumon Publishing. *My Book of Money: Dollars and Cents*. Teaneck, N.J.: Kumon Publishing, 2007.

Web Sites

Aplusmath
   <http://www.aplusmath.com/cgi-bin/
   flashcards/money>

Apples4theteacher: Practice Counting Money Game: Using Quarters, Dimes, Nickels and Pennies
   <http://www.apples4theteacher.com/java/counting/money.html>

INDEX

b
bills, 18–19
and coins, 20–21

c
coins, 4–17, 20–21
dimes, 5, 8–9

nickels, 4, 6–7
pennies, 4
quarters, 5, 10–11
counting
bills, 18–19
like coins, 4–5

different coins, 6–7
over a dollar, 16–17

d
decimal point, 16
dollar sign, 16

dollars, 16

m
make an amount, 12–13, 14–15

Enslow Elementary, an imprint of Enslow Publishers, Inc.
Enslow Elementary® is a registered trademark of Enslow Publishers, Inc.

Copyright © 2009 by Enslow Publishers, Inc.

All rights reserved.

No part of this book may be reproduced by any means without the written permission of the publisher.

Library of Congress Cataloging-in-Publication Data

Wingard-Nelson, Rebecca
    I can count money / Rebecca Wingard-Nelson
        p. cm. — (I like money math!)
    Summary: "An introduction to counting money for young readers"—Provided by publisher.
    Includes bibliographical references and index.
    ISBN 978-0-7660-3142-5
    1. Counting—Juvenile literature. 2. Money—United States—Juvenile literature.
I. Title.
    QA113.W5865 2010
    513.2'11—dc22   2009006489

Printed in the United States of America
052010 Lake Book Manufacturing, Inc., Melrose Park, IL

10 9 8 7 6 5 4 3 2

ISBN-13: 978-0-7660-3658-1 (paperback)
ISBN-10: 0-7660-3658-8 (paperback)

Photo Credits: Dave Watts/NHPA/Photoshot

Cover Photo: Shutterstock

Enslow Elementary
an imprint of
Enslow Publishers, Inc.
40 Industrial Road
Box 398
Berkeley Heights, NJ 07922
USA
http://www.enslow.com